## Using an embroidery hoop

Many embroiderers work successfully without using a hoop but I always use one. Doing so means that the fabric is held taut so you achieve a good tension easily by letting each stitch sit in place on the fabric. A traditional wooden hoop large enough to allow you to work a motif at a time is suitable. Be sure that in placing it other areas of stitching are not damaged. It will not matter if the hoop sits over existing stitches whilst you are working but be sure to remove the hoop at the end of each stitching session so that they can recover.

## Cross stitch

Each square on a chart represents one cross stitch worked over one square of Aida fabric or two threads each way on evenweave fabric. The colour to use is indicated by the symbol in the chart square and can be identified from the key. The centre of each chart is marked with two small arrows at the sides.

To start a piece of work, identify the colour required for the central stitch and commence stitching in the centre of the fabric, leaving an end long enough to darn into the back of the work later, or positioning the thread beneath the fabric so that the first few stitches will cover it.

Work cross stitches as shown depending on the type of fabric you are using. It is important that all top stitches lie in the same direction.

Cross stitch on Aida fabric

It is preferable to cross all stitches as you go rather than work rows of the first part of the stitch returning over them later as this can form a ridged line.

Cross stitch on evenweave fabric

Fasten off and begin your stitching by passing threads for about an inch through the wrong side of worked stitches. When finishing, cut the ends very close to the back of the work.

## Back stitch

Always complete the cross stitch before working back stitch.

Each back stitch is worked along one side of a square of Aida, or diagonally across a square as shown on the chart for the particular design.

On evenweave fabrics, the stitch is usually worked across two threads of the fabric.

## Sewing with beads

When stitching with beads the most important thing to remember is to change the needle you are using. A size 24 tapestry needle is usually used for cross stitch but the long eye is just a little too wide to fit through the hole in a seed bead. A bead embroidery needle is recommended for sewing on beads as the eye is small enough to fit through.

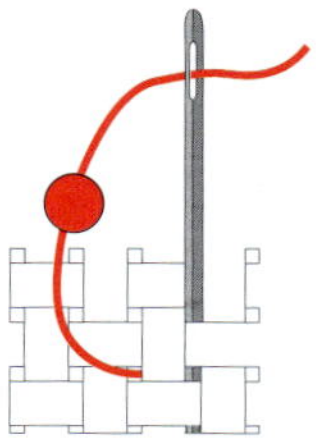

On Aida fabric sew the beads across the diagonal of the square of the fabric.

Fasten off the beading thread at the back of your work every few beads or so in case the thread breaks.

## Washing and pressing

When your embroidery is complete, it can be washed in soapy water and thoroughly rinsed. Press it between two clean towels to remove excess water and leave it to dry in natural or room heat.

When nearly dry, iron it carefully and lightly on the wrong side with the right side resting on a well-padded surface - an ordinary bath towel is good.

## Mounting in cards

Trim the embroidery to slightly less than the size of the card.

Place the embroidery face up on a clean surface. Test the position of the card over it. Now open up the card and run a trail of craft glue about ¼ inch in from the window on the inside of the card.

Be careful not to take the glue too near the edge of the cut-out area.

Turn the card over, check that it is the right way up and gently lower it into position on the embroidery. With dark coloured cards you may find that you need to stick a piece of white paper behind the embroidery so that the colour of the card does not show through.

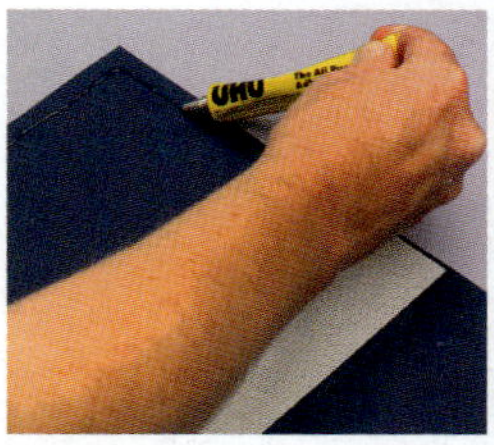


On the wrong side of the card run a trail of glue around the edge of the front flap, and fold this in behind the embroidery. Ensure the edges stick well.

If the thought of using glue to complete your cards makes you nervous, double-sided sticky tape is a perfectly acceptable alternative.

# *Shepherds, Nativity Scene and Three Kings*

The main part of each design is worked on white 14 count Aida fabric and mounted into a card. To give a three-dimensional effect, an element of each design is stitched on perforated paper and attached using craft foam pads.

## For each card you will need...

- ✓ Stranded cottons as listed.
- ✓ Kreinik gold very fine braid (shade 002).
- ✓ Tapestry needle size 24.
- ✓ Zweigart white 14 count Aida 10 x 8 ins (25 x 20 cms).
- ✓ White 14 count perforated paper. YT004
- ✓ Crafty Things brass cross charm. CT005
- ✓ Glue Dots craft foam pads. GD001
- ✓ Craft Creations extra large dark blue card, rectangular aperture 3¾ x 5¾ ins (9.5 x 14.7 cms). CC362/4
- ✓ Small stars from Craft Creations Santa, Stocking and Gifts gold sticker. CCT11

Choose from a wide selection of special charms for a unique finishing touch.

## Getting started...

- ☆ Find the chart for the Nativity Scene on page 16, the Three Kings on page 17 and the Shepherds on page 18.
- ☆ On the white 14 count Aida, Cross stitch all the design except for the crucifixes and the highlight (the sheep, the stable or the gifts, depending on which design you are working). Work all the cross stitches before working any Back stitch.
- ☆ Attach the brass cross charm in the position marked on the chart by a pink circle using the very fine braid.
- ☆ Mount the embroidery in the card in the usual way.
- ☆ On the white perforated paper, Cross stitch the highlight (the sheep, the stable or the gifts). Cut out the highlight leaving a one square gap around the stitching.
- ☆ Using the craft foam pads attach the highlight in position on the card. Finally stick the small gold stars around the card mount.

## *Festive Santa*

### You will need...

- ✓ Stranded cottons as listed.
- ✓ Kreinik red (shade 003) and gold (shade 002) blending filament.
- ✓ Tapestry needle size 24.
- ✓ White 14 count perforated paper. YT004
- ✓ Craft Glue Dots. GD002
- ✓ Craft Creations silver metallic three panel card, each panel 4 x 6 ins (10.4 x 15.2 cms). CCB04
- ✓ Fiskars Shapecutter. FK005
- ✓ Fiskars Squares template. FK004
- ✓ Making Memories Ribbon Words 'tis the season ribbon. TC020
- ✓ Craft Creations gold Merry Christmas sticker. CCT13
- ✓ Craft Creations red Alchemy paper. CCP02

### Getting started...

☆ Find the chart for the Festive Santa on page 17.

☆ Cross stitch the design on white perforated paper.

☆ Glue the Santa onto a piece of red Alchemy paper and cut it out leaving a one square gap around the stitching. Cut through both the perforated paper and red backing paper.

☆ Remove a panel from the three panel card to make a single fold card and cut a 2 ins (5 cms) square aperture in the front panel using the Fiskars Shapecutter and Squares template.

☆ Attach Santa to the edge of the aperture using a couple of Craft Glue Dots, stick a Merry Christmas sticker through the aperture and add the 'tis the season ribbon to the front.

## *Christmas Tree*

### You will need...

- ✓ Stranded cottons as listed.
- ✓ Kreinik gold very fine braid (shade 002).
- ✓ Kreinik green blending filament (shade 008).
- ✓ Bead embroidery needle .
- ✓ Red and gold seed beads.
- ✓ Tapestry needle size 24.
- ✓ Zweigart opalescent (shade 11) 14 count Aida 5 x 6 ins (13 x 15 cms).
- ✓ Craft Creations small dark blue card, rectangular aperture 2¼ x 1¾ ins (5.8 x 4.4 cms). CC378/6
- ✓ Dovecraft Handcrafted Embellishments Christmas Candy present. TC003

### Getting started...

☆ Find the chart for the Christmas Tree on page 19.

☆ Cross stitch the tree on the opalescent Aida. Then sew on the beads.

☆ Mount the embroidery in the card in the usual way and stick the present embellishment onto the card.

# *Border and Tree*

## You will need...

- ✓ Stranded cottons as listed.
- ✓ Tapestry needle size 24.
- ✓ Kreinik gold blending filament (shade 002).
- ✓ Zweigart royal blue (shade 567) 14 count Aida 7 ins (18 cms) square.
- ✓ Card Art large white card, aperture 2⅞ ins (7.2 cms) square. SB186/6
- ✓ Dovecraft Handcrafted Embellishment, Christmas Ornaments tree. TC001

## Getting started...

☆ Find the chart for the Square Border on page 17.

☆ Cross stitch the border on the royal blue Aida.

☆ Mount the embroidery in the card in the usual way and stick the tree embellishment in the centre of the fabric.

# *Season's Greetings*

## You will need...

- ✓ Stranded cottons as listed.
- ✓ Tapestry needle size 24.
- ✓ Zweigart navy (shade 589) 14 count Aida, 9 x 7 ins (23 x 18 cms).
- ✓ Gold 14 count perforated paper. YT001
- ✓ Glue Dots craft foam pads. GD001
- ✓ Craft Creations linen gloss gold card, oval aperture 3 x 4½ ins (7.5 x 11.3 cms). CC1468/6

## Getting started...

☆ Find the chart for the Season's Greetings design on page 16.

☆ On the navy 14 count Aida, Cross stitch the holly design but omit the greetings scroll.

☆ Mount the embroidery in the card in the usual way.

☆ On the gold perforated paper, Cross stitch the greetings scroll. Work all the Cross stitch before the Back stitch. Cut out the scroll leaving a one square gap around the stitching.

☆ Using several craft foam pads attach the scroll in the centre of the design.

# Snowman card 1

## You will need...

- ✓ Stranded cottons as listed.
- ✓ Kreinik pearl blending filament (shade 032).
- ✓ Tapestry needle size 24.
- ✓ Zweigart light blue (shade 503) 14 count Aida 7 ins (18 cms) square.
- ✓ Craft Creations medium deep green card, aperture 2 ins (5 cms) square. CC2441/6
- ✓ Craft Creations gold Happy Christmas sticker. CCT23

## Getting started...

☆ Find the chart for the Snowman on page 19.

☆ Cross stitch the snowman on the light blue Aida.

☆ Mount the embroidery in the card in the usual way and stick the Happy Christmas and holly stickers on the card.

Add greetings in an instant with these lovely plaques for your cards, inside and out.

# Winter Friends

## Getting started...

☆ Find the charts for the Winter Friends design on page 18.

☆ Cross stitch the design on the white Aida.

☆ Using the Fiskars Shapecutter and Circles template cut a 2 ins (5 cms) aperture around the existing square aperture of the deep green card to fit the design.

☆ Before mounting the embroidery in the card, use the Fiskars Shapeboss embossing system and Christmas stencil to emboss some holly in the bottom corner of the card.

☆ Mount the embroidery in the card and attach the Merry Christmas plaque to the front.

## You will need...

- ✓ Stranded cottons as listed.
- ✓ Tapestry needle size 24.
- ✓ Zweigart white 14 count Aida 5 ins (13 cms) square.
- ✓ Craft Creations tall deep green card, aperture 1⅜ ins (3.5 cms) square. CC2450/6
- ✓ Fiskars Shapecutter. FK005
- ✓ Fiskars Circles template. FK001
- ✓ Fiskars Shapeboss embossing system. FK021
- ✓ Fiskars Christmas embossing stencil. FK033
- ✓ Making Memories Charmed Words Merry Christmas plaque. TC010

## *Snowman card 2*

### You will need...

- ✓ Stranded cottons as listed.
- ✓ Kreinik pearl blending filament (shade 032).
- ✓ Tapestry needle size 24.
- ✓ Red 14 count perforated paper. YT003
- ✓ Craft Glue Dots. GD002
- ✓ Craft Creations deep green three panel card, each panel 4 x 6 ins (10.4 x 15.2 cms). CCB02
- ✓ Christmas coloured paper/card for backing, we used red and gold.
- ✓ Craft Creations silver Merry Christmas sticker. CCT14
- ✓ Fiskars snowflake border punch. FK013

### Getting started...

- ☆ Find the chart for the Snowman on page 19.
- ☆ Cross stitch the snowman on the red perforated paper.
- ☆ Cut out the snowman leaving a one square gap around the stitching.
- ☆ Remove a panel from the three panel card to make a single fold card and punch a snowflake border along the right hand edge of the front panel using the Fiskars border punch.
- ☆ Cut a piece of gold card just large enough for the snowman to sit inside and then cut a piece of red card slightly larger again.
- ☆ Stick the snowman to the gold card, the gold card to the red card and then position on the front panel of the card.
- ☆ Stick the Merry Christmas sticker to the front of the card.

# HOW TO... emboss cards

*It's easy to add an embossed motif to a plain card with the Fiskars Shapeboss. Follow these step by step instructions to give a three-dimensional touch to your cards.*

These pegs hold the dual-layer stencil securely in place.

Dual-tip stylus with one fine and one standard nib.

Make a plain card extra special with a touch of embossing.

To create lots of different effects, you'll need a supply of stencils. These ones come in two parts that are slightly offset to give crisp embossed edges to your motifs.

The easy way to emboss is with a Fiskars Shapeboss system.

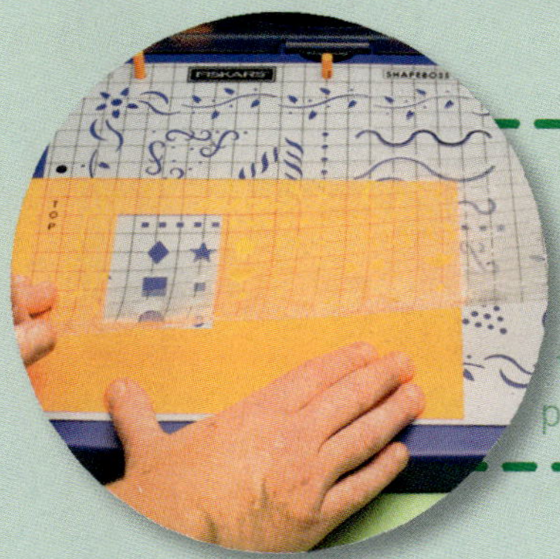

**1** Peg in the two stencils and place the card face down over the motif, using the grid to help position it correctly.

**2** Pressing down to keep the card in place, use the stylus and 'draw' around the edge of the stencil motif. Use even pressure and the finer end for motifs with tight corners.

# Robin and Mistletoe

## You will need...

- ✓ Stranded cottons as listed.
- ✓ Kreinik gold very fine braid (shade 002).
- ✓ Tapestry needle size 24.
- ✓ Bead embroidery needle.
- ✓ White seed beads.
- ✓ Zweigart white 14 count Aida 3 ins (7 cms) square.
- ✓ Red 14 count perforated paper. YT003
- ✓ Craft Glue Dots. GD002
- ✓ Craft Creations small bright yellow card aperture 1½ ins (4 cms) square. CC2447/6

## Getting started...

- ☆ Find the chart for the Mistletoe border on page 18 and the Robin on page 15.
- ☆ On the white 14 count Aida, Cross stitch the Robin.
- ☆ Mount the embroidery in the card in the usual way.
- ☆ On the red perforated paper, Cross stitch the border from the Mistletoe & Candle design (omitting the candle).
- ☆ Cut out the border leaving a one square gap around the stitching. Using a few Glue Dots attach the border to the card centrally over the robin.

# Stocking and Holly

## You will need...

- ✓ Stranded cottons as listed.
- ✓ Kreinik gold very fine braid (shade 002).
- ✓ Tapestry needle size 24.
- ✓ Zweigart red (shade 954) 14 count Aida 7 ins (18 cms) square.
- ✓ Craft Creations small bright green card aperture 2½ ins (6.3 cms) square. CC216/6
- ✓ Making Memories Charmed Plaque Christmas stocking. TC009

## Getting started...

- ☆ Find the chart for the holly border on the Lantern design on page 15.
- ☆ Cross stitch the border from the Lantern design on the red 14 count Aida fabric (omitting the lantern).
- ☆ Mount the embroidery in the card in the usual way and stick the stocking plaque in the centre of the fabric.

# Lantern

## You will need...

- ✓ Stranded cottons as listed.
- ✓ Kreinik gold very fine braid (shade 002).
- ✓ Tapestry needle size 24.
- ✓ Zweigart red (shade 954) 18 count Aida 5 ins (13 cms) square.
- ✓ Red 14 count perforated paper. YT003
- ✓ Glue Dots craft foam pads. GD001
- ✓ A three panel card, each panel 3½ x 4½ ins (8.9 x 11.4 cms) made from a piece of card from the Craft Creations Stardream Multipack. CCP04
- ✓ Fiskars Shapeboss embossing system. FK021
- ✓ Fiskars Shapeboss Christmas stencil. FK033
- ✓ Fiskars Shapecutter. FK005
- ✓ Fiskars Squares template. FK004

## Getting started...

☆ Find the chart for the Lantern on page 15.

☆ Cross stitch the lantern on the red 18 count Aida fabric

☆ On the red perforated paper, Cross stitch the green holly border. Cut out the border leaving a one square gap around the stitching.

☆ Using the Fiskars Shapecutter and Squares template cut a 1½ ins (3.8 cms) square aperture in the centre panel of the card.

☆ Using the Fiskars Shapeboss embossing system and Christmas stencil add a holly motif to the bottom corner of the card.

☆ Mount the embroidery in the card in the usual way and, using the craft foam pads, attach the perforated paper border to the card, centrally over the lantern.

# Mistletoe & Candle

## You will need...

- ✓ Stranded cottons as listed.
- ✓ Kreinik gold very fine braid (shade 002).
- ✓ Tapestry needle size 24.
- ✓ Bead embroidery needle.
- ✓ White seed beads.
- ✓ Zweigart red (shade 954) 14 count Aida, 7 ins (18 cms) square.
- ✓ Red 14 count perforated paper. YT003
- ✓ Glue Dots craft foam pads. GD001
- ✓ Craft Creations small linen gloss gold card, aperture 2½ ins (6 cms) square. CC1486/6

## Getting started...

☆ Find the chart for the Mistletoe and Candle on page 18.

☆ On the red 14 count Aida, Cross stitch the border design (omitting the candle).

☆ Mount the embroidery in the card in the usual way.

☆ On the red perforated paper, Cross stitch the candle. Cut out the candle leaving a one square gap around the stitching.

☆ Using a few craft foam pads, attach the candle in the centre of the design.

# Deep Blue Card

## Getting started...

- Find the chart for the santa's face on page 17 and the robin on page 19.
- Cross stitch the face of the Festive Santa and a robin from the Robins and Holly design on white perforated paper.
- Cut around each motif leaving a one square gap all round the stitching.
- Take a small square of pale blue paper and glue behind the aperture of the dark blue card.
- Stick the Santa motif in the centre of the aperture with a glue dot and stick the robin motif in the bottom corner using some craft foam pads.
- Stick the Happy Christmas sticker on the card.

## You will need...

- ✓ Stranded cottons as listed.
- ✓ Kreinik red (shade 003) blending filament.
- ✓ Tapestry needle size 24.
- ✓ White 14 count perforated paper. YT004
- ✓ Craft Creations dark blue card, aperture 1⅜ ins (3.5 cms) square. CC2483/6
- ✓ Glue Dots craft foam pads. GD001
- ✓ Craft Glue Dots. GD002
- ✓ Craft Creations pale blue Alchemy paper. CCP02
- ✓ Craft Creations gold Happy Christmas sticker. CCT23

Seed beads are available in so many colours and they are the perfect size to add sparkle to cross stitch!

# Tall Window Card

## You will need...

- ✓ Stranded cottons as listed.
- ✓ Kreinik red (shade 003) and green (shade 008) blending filament.
- ✓ Bead embroidery needle.
- ✓ Red, gold, green and white beads.
- ✓ Tapestry needle size 24.
- ✓ Silver 14 count perforated paper. YT002
- ✓ Craft Creations tall red card with 4 apertures, each aperture 1¼ ins (2.8 cms) square. CC2501/6

## Getting started...

- Find the chart for the bell, stocking and tree on page 15 and the santa's face on page 17.
- Cross stitch the designs on silver perforated paper leaving at least ½ inch (1.3 cms) around the edges of the motifs. Then sew on the beads.
- Cut out each motif and position centrally behind each window and glue into place.

## *Square Window Card*

### You will need...

- ✓ Stranded cottons as listed.
- ✓ Kreinik red (shade 003) and green (shade 008) blending filament.
- ✓ Bead embroidery needle.
- ✓ Red, gold, green and white beads.
- ✓ Tapestry needle size 24.
- ✓ Zweigart opalescent (shade 11) 14 count Aida 5 ins (12 cms) square.
- ✓ Craft Creations square hammer red card with 4 apertures, each aperture 1⅝ ins (4 cms) square. CC2461/6

### Getting started...

☆ Find the chart for the robin, bell, tree and stocking on page 15.

☆ Lay the fabric beneath the apertures of the card and mark the centre of each window on the fabric with a disappearing marker pen. Mark the middle of each square.

☆ Cross stitch each motif in the centre of each square, then sew the beads and mount the embroidery on the card in the usual way.

# HOW TO... cut apertures

***Cutting apertures neatly can be tricky, but it is simple with a Fiskars Shapecutter and templates. Follow these simple instructions to make aperture cards in an instant.***

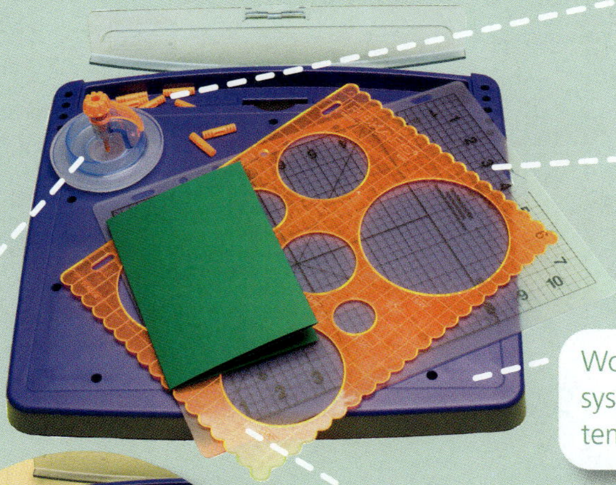

Pegs hold the craft mat and template securely in place.

Use a Fiskars craft mat to protect the surface of the Shapeboss.

Work on a Shapeboss system to prevent the template slipping.

The Shapecutter has a small blade in the centre of the holder to cut perfect apertures quickly and safely.

To cut accurate and neat apertures use a plastic template available with different-sized circle, oval, rectangular and square shapes.

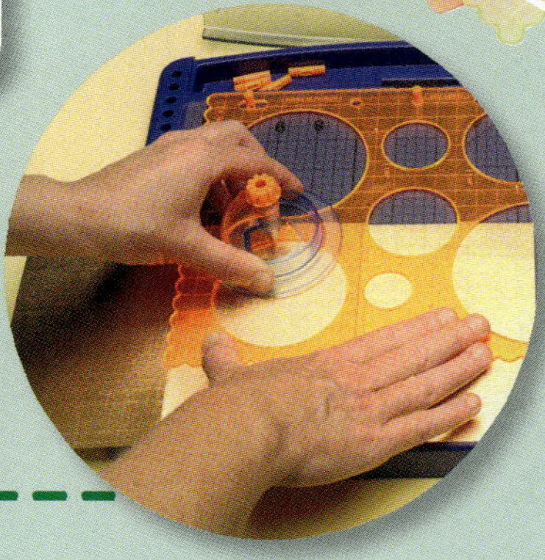

Pressing down to keep the card in place, run the Shapecutter around the edge of the aperture on the plastic template.

# Baubles

## You will need...

- ✓ Stranded cottons as listed.
- ✓ Kreinik gold very fine braid (shade 002).
- ✓ Tapestry needle size 24.
- ✓ Silver 14 count perforated paper. YT002
- ✓ Craft Creations extra large raspberry card, aperture 4 ins (10 cms) square. CC992/4
- ✓ Craft Creations gold Happy Christmas sticker. CCT23

## Getting started...

- ☆ Find the chart for the Baubles on page 19.
- ☆ Work all the Cross stitch before the Back stitch.
- ☆ Cut out the baubles leaving one square around the stitching.
- ☆ Draw around the square aperture on the inside of the card's left flap and use a craft knife and metal ruler to cut out a second aperture.
- ☆ Hang the baubles using very fine braid and attach inside the flap. Stick the Happy Christmas and candle stickers on the card.

# Robins and Holly

## You will need...

- ✓ Stranded cottons as listed.
- ✓ Tapestry needle size 24.
- ✓ Zweigart white 14 count Aida 8 ins (20 cms) square.
- ✓ White 14 count perforated paper. YT004
- ✓ Glue Dots craft foam pads. GD001
- ✓ Craft Creations medium bright green card, rectangular aperture 2¼ x 3ins (5.7 x 7.6 cms). CC212/6
- ✓ Craft Creations gold Bells, Trees and Candles sticker. CCT09

## Getting started...

- ☆ Find the chart for the Robins and Holly on page 19.
- ☆ Cross stitch the Robins and Holly design on the white Aida and mount in the card in the usual way.
- ☆ Cross stitch the upper robin motif from the chart onto a piece of white perforated paper.
- ☆ Cut around the robin one square away from the stitching and attach to the corner of the card using a craft foam pad.
- ☆ Stick the bell sticker on the card.

To use the 'negative' parts of a sticker that are left take a piece of low adhesive tape and place over the area to be removed. Rub with the side of your nail or the back of a spoon. Gently peel off the parts of the sticker to be moved. Place onto the card and repeat; smooth down with the spoon or your nail until the sticker is attached to the card. Gently remove the low adhesive tape.

# Cross stitch charts

On the following pages you'll find charts for all the designs in this book. Follow the step by step instructions given with each card on the previous pages.

## Robin

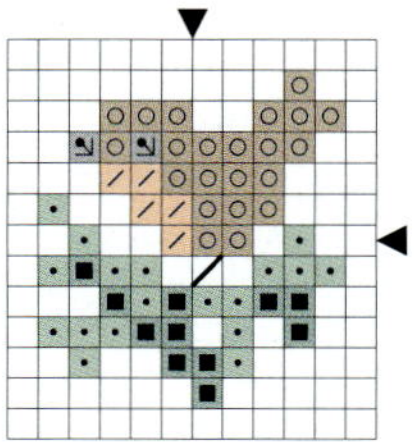

| | Anchor | DMC | ½metres |
|---|---|---|---|
| **Cross stitch in 2 strands** | | | |
| • | 210 | 562 | 1 |
| ⁄ | 332 | 946 | 1 |
| ○ | 358 | 801 | 1 |
| ↘ | 403 | 310 | 1 |
| ■ | 212 | 561 | 1 |
| **Back stitch in 1 strand** | | | |
| — | 403 | 310 | 1 |

**Design count:**
7 sts wide x 11 sts high

**Design size** (14 count Aida):
0.5 x 0.8 ins (1.3 x 2.0 cms)

## Tiny Tree

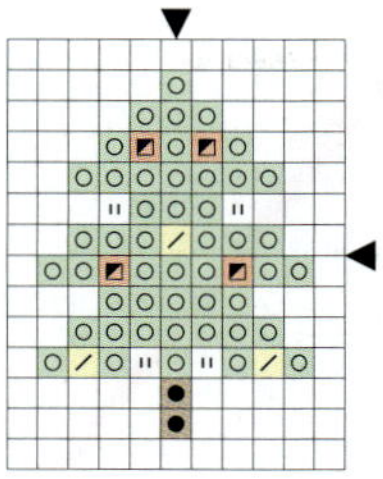

| | Anchor | DMC | ½metres |
|---|---|---|---|
| **Cross stitch in 2 strands** | | | |
| ● | 944 | 869 | 1 |
| **Cross stitch in 2 strands + green blending filament** | | | |
| ○ | 226 | 702 | 1 |
| **Beads** | | | |
| ◪ | red | | |
| ıı | white | | |
| ⁄ | gold | | |

**Design count:**
9 sts wide x 12 sts high

**Design size** (14 count Aida):
0.6 x 0.8 ins (1.6 x 2.1 cms)

## Tiny Stocking

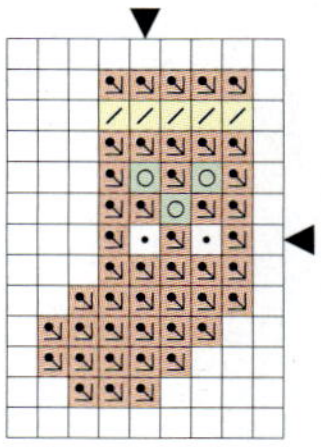

| | Anchor | DMC | ½metres |
|---|---|---|---|
| **Cross stitch in 2 strands** | | | |
| ⁄ | 290 | 973 | 1 |
| **Cross stitch in 2 strands + red blending filament** | | | |
| ↘ | 46 | 666 | 1 |
| **Beads** | | | |
| • | white | | |
| ○ | green | | |

**Design count:**
7 sts wide x 11 sts high

**Design size** (14 count Aida):
0.5 x 0.8 ins (1.3 x 2.0 cms)

## Lantern

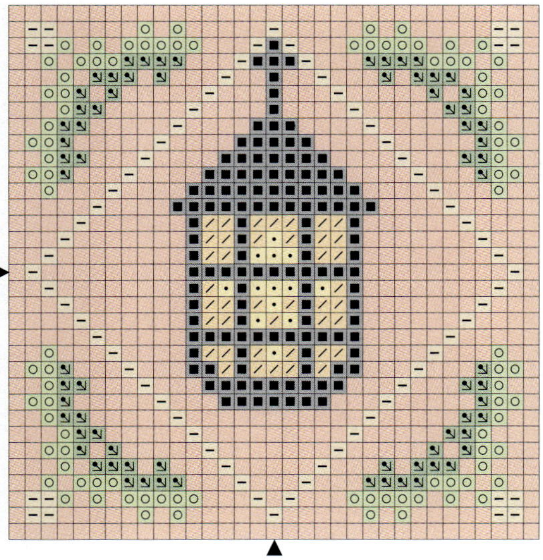

| | Anchor | DMC | ½metres |
|---|---|---|---|
| **Cross stitch in 2 strands** | | | |
| • | 297 | 973 | 1 |
| ⁄ | 314 | 741 | 1 |
| ○ | 255 | 907 | 2 |
| ↘ | 258 | 905 | 1 |
| ■ | 403 | 310 | 2 |
| **Cross stitch in very fine braid** | | | |
| – | - | - | 4 |

**Design count:**
31 sts wide x 31 sts high

**Design size** (18 count Aida):
2.2 x 2.2 ins (5.6 x 5.6 cms)

## Christmas Bell

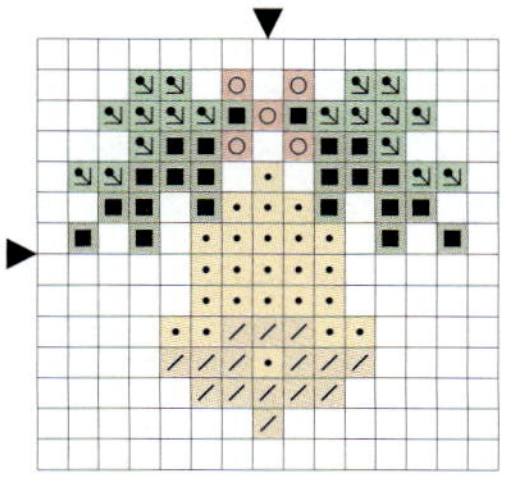

| | Anchor | DMC | ½metres |
|---|---|---|---|
| **Cross stitch in 2 strands + gold blending filament** | | | |
| • | 891 | 676 | 1 |
| ⁄ | 890 | 729 | 1 |
| **Cross stitch in 2 strands + green blending filament** | | | |
| ↘ | 227 | 701 | 1 |
| ■ | 246 | 986 | 1 |
| **Beads** | | | |
| ○ | red | | |

**Design count:** 13 sts wide x 12 sts high

**Design size on 14 count Aida**
0.9 x 0.8 ins (2.4 x 2.2 cms)

# *Season's Greetings*

| | Anchor | DMC | ½metres |
|---|---|---|---|
| **Cross stitch in 2 strands** | | | |
| • | 214 | 966 | 1 |
| / | 216 | 320 | 2 |
| ○ | 332 | 946 | 1 |
| ↘ | 46 | 666 | 1 |
| ■ | 218 | 561 | 2 |
| – | 390 | 3866 | 2 |
| ↓ | 391 | 3033 | 4 |
| ↘ | 392 | 642 | 2 |
| ◩ | 393 | 640 | 1 |
| ● | 246 | 986 | 2 |
| ıı | 242 | 989 | 1 |
| Y | 244 | 701 | 2 |
| **Back stitch in 2 strands** | | | |
| ▬ | 403 | 310 | 1 |
| **Back stitch in 1 strand** | | | |
| ▬ | 360 | 898 | 1 |

**Design count:**
48 sts wide x 32 sts high

**Design size** (14 count Aida):
3.4 x 2.3 ins (8.7 x 5.8 cms)

# *Nativity Scene*

| | Anchor | DMC | ½metres |
|---|---|---|---|
| **Cross stitch in 2 strands** | | | |
| • | 1 | B5200 | 1 |
| / | 397 | 3072 | 2 |
| ○ | 399 | 415 | 4 |
| ↘ | 235 | 414 | 2 |
| ■ | 403 | 310 | 1 |
| – | 128 | 3753 | 2 |
| ↓ | 130 | 809 | 2 |
| ↘ | 131 | 798 | 2 |
| ◩ | 133 | 796 | 1 |
| ● | 149 | 336 | 1 |
| ıı | 1080 | 842 | 1 |
| Y | 303 | 742 | 1 |
| × | 1024 | 3328 | 1 |
| ш | 1025 | 347 | 1 |
| ▲ | 22 | 815 | 1 |
| L | 890 | 729 | 2 |
| ⌀ | 256 | 906 | 1 |
| ✳ | 245 | 701 | 1 |
| ◘ | 1086 | 3781 | 2 |
| ⋱ | 347 | 402 | 1 |
| > | 349 | 301 | 1 |
| **Cross stitch in very fine braid** | | | |
| ⋰ | - | - | 2 |
| **Back stitch in very fine braid** | | | |
| ▬ | - | - | 1 |
| **Back stitch in 1 strand** | | | |
| ▬ | 403 | 310 | 1 |

**Design count:**
47 sts wide x 77 sts high

**Design size** (14 count Aida):
3.3 x 5.5 ins (8.5 x 14 cms)

# Three Kings

| | Anchor | DMC | ½metres |
|---|---|---|---|
| **Cross stitch in 2 strands** | | | |
| • | 1080 | 842 | 1 |
| / | 399 | 415 | 1 |
| ○ | 1086 | 3781 | 1 |
| ↘ | 245 | 701 | 1 |
| ■ | 403 | 310 | 1 |
| ↓ | 256 | 906 | 1 |
| ↘ | 334 | 606 | 3 |
| ◩ | 112 | 333 | 2 |
| ● | 102 | 550 | 3 |
| ıı | 303 | 742 | 2 |
| Y | 131 | 798 | 1 |
| × | 925 | 740 | 3 |
| ш | 133 | 796 | 1 |
| ▲ | 47 | 321 | 4 |
| **Cross stitch in very fine braid** | | | |
| – | - | - | 2 |
| **Back stitch in very fine braid** | | | |
| — | - | - | 1 |

**Design count:**
77sts wide x 47 sts high

**Design size** (14 count Aida):
5.5 x 3.3 ins (14 x 8.5 cms)

# Festive Santa

| | Anchor | DMC | ½metres |
|---|---|---|---|
| **Cross stitch in 2 strands** | | | |
| • | 1 | B5200 | 1 |
| / | 778 | 3774 | 1 |
| ■ | 403 | 310 | 1 |
| **Cross stitch in 2 strands + red blending filament** | | | |
| ↘ | 46 | 666 | 3 |
| **Cross stitch in 2 strands + gold blending filament** | | | |
| ○ | 874 | 834 | 1 |

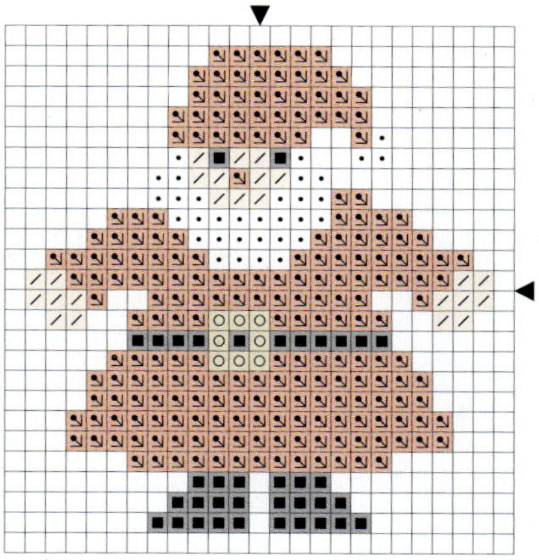

**Design count:**
23 sts wide x 24 sts high

**Design size** (14 count Aida):
1.6 x 1.7 ins (4.1 x 4.4 cms)

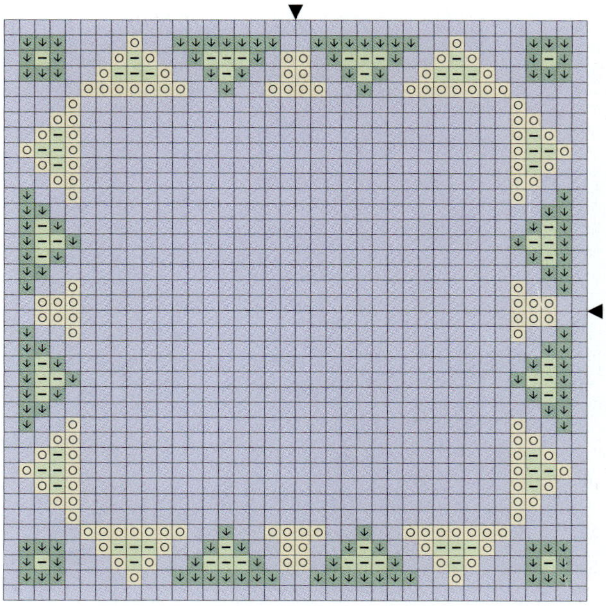

# Square Border

| | Anchor | DMC | ½metres |
|---|---|---|---|
| **Cross stitch in 2 strands** | | | |
| – | 255 | 907 | 2 |
| ↓ | 245 | 701 | 2 |
| **Cross stitch in 2 strands + blending filament** | | | |
| ○ | 874 | 834 | 2 |

**Design count:**
36 sts wide x 36 sts high

**Design size** (14 count Aida):
2.6 x 2.6 ins (6.5 x 6.5 cms)

# Shepherds

| | Anchor | DMC | ½metres |
|---|---|---|---|
| **Cross stitch in 2 strands** | | | |
| • | 926 | 712 | 1 |
| ○ | 399 | 415 | 1 |
| ◣ | 22 | 815 | 1 |
| ■ | 403 | 310 | 1 |
| – | 928 | 3761 | 1 |
| ↓ | 130 | 809 | 1 |
| ➘ | 168 | 807 | 1 |
| ◩ | 169 | 806 | 1 |
| ● | 164 | 517 | 1 |
| ॥ | 1080 | 842 | 1 |
| Y | 347 | 402 | 1 |
| × | 349 | 301 | 1 |
| ш | 355 | 975 | 1 |
| ▲ | 359 | 801 | 1 |
| ⋰ | 240 | 368 | 1 |
| L | 242 | 989 | 1 |
| ⌀ | 245 | 701 | 1 |
| ✳ | 1044 | 895 | 1 |
| **Cross stitch in very fine braid** | | | |
| / | - | - | 2 |
| **Back stitch in very fine braid** | | | |
| — (gold) | - | - | 1 |
| **Back stitch in 1 strand** | | | |
| — (black) | 403 | 310 | 1 |
| — (brown) | 1082 | 841 | 1 |

**Design count:** 77 sts wide x 47 sts high

**Design size** (14 count Aida):
5.5 x 3.3 ins (14 x 8.5 cms)

# Winter Friends

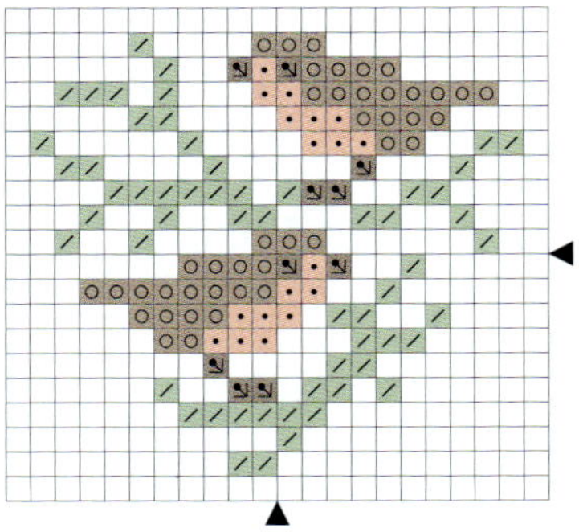

| | Anchor | DMC | ½metres |
|---|---|---|---|
| **Cross stitch in 2 strands** | | | |
| • | 1098 | 3801 | 1 |
| / | 258 | 904 | 1 |
| ○ | 360 | 898 | 1 |
| ◣ | 382 | 3371 | 1 |

**Design count:**
20 sts wide x 18 sts high

**Design size** (14 count Aida):
1.4 x 1.2 ins (3.6 x 3.3 cms)

# Mistletoe & Candle

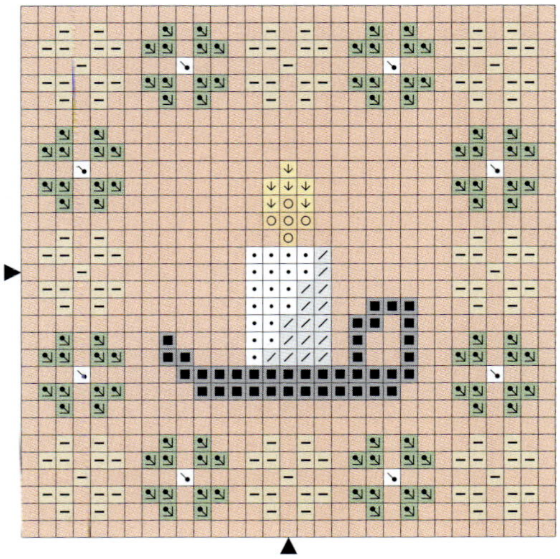

| | Anchor | DMC | ½metres |
|---|---|---|---|
| **Cross stitch in 2 strands** | | | |
| • | 1 | B5200 | 1 |
| / | 234 | 762 | 1 |
| ○ | 314 | 741 | 1 |
| ◣ | 258 | 905 | 2 |
| ■ | 403 | 310 | 1 |
| ↓ | 297 | 973 | 1 |
| **Cross stitch in very fine braid** | | | |
| – | - | - | 5 |
| **Beads** | | | |
| ➘ | white | | |

**Design count:**
29 sts wide x 29 sts high

**Design size** (14 count Aida):
2.1 x 2.1 ins (5.3 x 5.3 cms)